My Beginners Book 1

Fun Pre-Suzuki Violin School Volume 1 Method
Takes Beginners to Prep Test Level

Students' Book

Violin

Luisa Faraguna

SECOND EDITION
from 2014

To be purchased separately:
- CD1 Performance Tracks
- CD2 Backing Tracks
- Piano Accompaniment Book (it includes score with piano part and chord symbols for other accompanying instruments)

Book text, design, illustrations and music origination by Luisa Faraguna
CDs piano, violin performance and edition by Luisa Faraguna
Further information at: www.wimbledonmusicschool.co.uk
Cover Design by Virginia Chiappa
Published by Music Seekers Publishing Ltd. UK
Copyright © 2011 Luisa Faraguna. All rights reserved.
ISBN 978 0 9571086 0 8

Author's Note

My Beginners' Book 1 includes 16 progressive tunes and games from the very first lesson up to Prep Test standard. The book and CD teaches musical understanding, technical dexterity and posture. Students will be singing, clapping, stepping on time, playing and transposing from the very first day of lessons.

These highly successful teaching methods have been especially created and combined to support Violin Group Tuition in Primary Schools. Nevertheless, it is suitable for any teacher or parent who wishes their pupils, children or themselves to learn to play the fiddle. It is designed to develop musicianship at the same time as learning the basics of violin technique.

My Beginners Book 1 will guide teachers and parents in achieving the best possible results from the student's home practice. No previous musical knowledge is required. There are 2 supplementary CDs (performance and play along tracks) and Piano Accompaniment Book that are strongly recommended to support the child's learning. These can be purchased separately.

In order to ensure that students acquire a good posture and start their ear training in an effective way, notation is only minimally introduced at this early stage of music education. Therefore, the CDs are the main learning tool for the students. Whereas the book is to be used by teachers and parents for supporting their learning.

Having fun during the learning process is the first key to unlock pupils' musical potential. I have compiled a number of games and tunes that can be combined in multiple ways to make home practice more entertaining and a different experience every single time. Ear training is deeply connected to singing so you will find that most of the songs have lyrics to sing along with before learning how to play them on the violin. An important technique for learning is 'singing with finger numbers'. This combines the visual, auditory and finger movement memory to cement different songs and how to play them on the violin in the child's mind.

The second key to unlock pupils' musical potential is clever repetition, particularly through home practice. Home practice will allow students to enjoy every single lesson by creating a feeling of progress and personal satisfaction. Listening to the CDs, especially to the performance tracks as much as possible is a great idea to get familiar with the musical material before playing it. Home practice allows students to better retain the physical skills and musical knowledge taught in lessons.

Violin is an exciting novelty in a student's life and even the youngest of learners will soon associate this CD with activities from their violin lessons. They will love showing off and demonstrating what they already know. Home performance in front of family is highly encouraged and appreciated by all!

After finishing *My Beginners Book I*, students will have a solid technique and a basic musical knowledge that will allow them to take the next step in their violin training. I hope you will enjoy it. Good luck and go for it!

Luisa Faraguna, London 2011

CDs Index

CD 1 - Performance Tracks

1. My Human Being Violin
2. Pop! Goes the Weasel
3. The Rocket Song
4. Tasty Soup
5. Witches & Wizards Brew
6. Funk Pluck
7. eTunes Watermelon
8. eTune Strawberry
9. eTune Apple
10. eTune Pear
11. eTune Lemonade
12. eTune Blackcurrant
13. eTune Margherita Pizza
14. eTune This is How We End
15. aTunes Watermelon
16. aTune Strawberry
17. aTune Apple
18. aTune Pear
19. aTune Lemonade
20. aTune Blackcurrant
21. aTune Margherita Pizza
22. aTune This is How We End
23. Rhythm of the Strings
24. Straight Rock & Roll
25. Learning to Play
26. Brazilian Samba
27. Monkey Song (E String)
28. Monkey Song (A String)
29. Pease Pudding (E String)
30. Pease Pudding (A String)
31. Twinkle Twinkle Little Star
32. Old MacDonald
33. A Major Scale Song

CD 2 - Backing Tracks

1. My Human Being Violin
2. Pop! Goes the Weasel
3. The Rocket Song
4. Tasty Soup
5. Witches & Wizards Brew
6. Funk Pluck
7. eTunes Watermelon
8. eTune Strawberry
9. eTune Apple
10. eTune Pear
11. eTune Lemonade
12. eTune Blackcurrant
13. eTune Margherita Pizza
14. eTune This is How We End
15. aTunes Watermelon
16. aTune Strawberry
17. aTune Apple
18. aTune Pear
19. aTune Lemonade
20. aTune Blackcurrant
21. aTune Margherita Pizza
22. aTune This is How We End
23. Rhythm of the Strings
24. Freezing Rock & Roll Game
25. Learning to Play
26. Brazilian Samba
27. Monkey Song (E String)
28. Monkey Song (A String)
29. Pease Pudding (E String)
30. Pease Pudding (A String)
31. Twinkle Twinkle Little Star
32. Old MacDonald
33. A Major Scale Song

Book Index

My Beginners Book 1 - from Beginner to Prep Test Level in 16 songs

Chapter 1: Vocabulary & Presentations

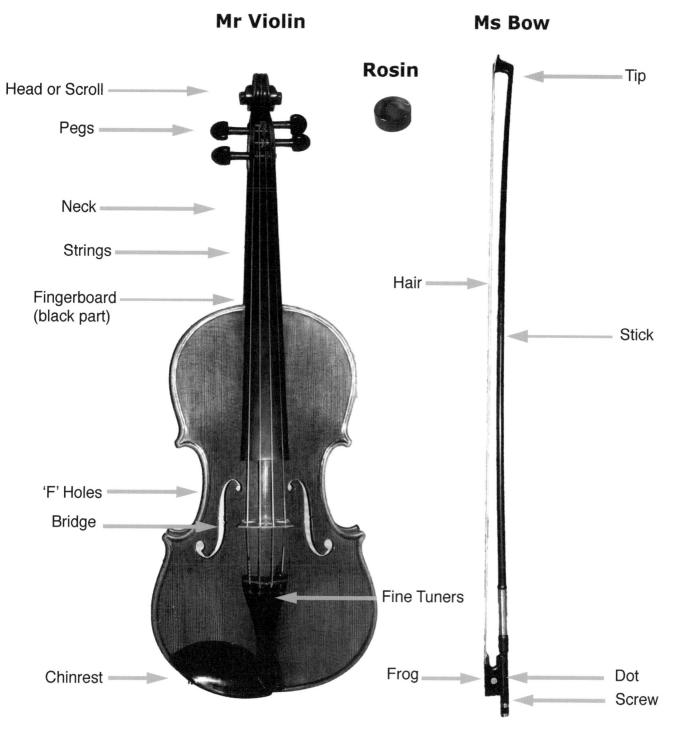

Mr Violin

Ms Bow

Rosin

Head or Scroll

Pegs

Neck

Strings

Fingerboard
(black part)

'F' Holes

Bridge

Chinrest

Tip

Hair

Stick

Fine Tuners

Frog

Dot

Screw

Magic Rules

1. **Mr Violin** likes lying down on his back and never on his belly. Its bridge is very delicate and cannot touch the floor in any case.
2. **Mr Bow** has sticky hair! It is actually pony tail covered with sticky Rosin powder. Please, do not touch it or you will get white stained sticky fingers.
3. **Rosin** is to be used to soup the bow's hair. No rosin equal no sound. Please, ask your teacher or a skilled adult to rosin your bow once a week.

My Human Being Violin

Composer: Luisa Faraguna

Track 1
CD

Activity

1. Unzip your violin case
2. Seat down in front of your violin and look carefully
3. What can you see?
4. Listen to Track 1 on the CD once
5. Listen it again and now try to sing with the lyrics
6. Learn the Violin Part Names while you point at them
7. Play the 'Where is it? Game' with Parents and Friends to test your memory skills

Learning Points

- Memorising the violin part names as much as possible to be able to follow the teacher's instructions during lessons
- Getting familiar with the anatomy of your new instrument
- Improving your listening skills and your capacity to relate auditory and visual content
- Singing a song along with the teacher and/or CD
- How many chorus and verses are there in the song? Starting to think about the structure of songs

Chapter 2: Posture

Rest Position

1. Your Violin is like a Baby, be careful not to drop it

2. Hold the violin's neck with your left hand

3. Mr Straight (your left hand Thumb) lives between the 2 white stickers

4. Your Elbow should lean on the top of the Chinrest

5. Make sure your strings are free to ring

6. Bow hanging from your right index and pointing to the floor

7. Feet Together!

Playing Position

Step 1: To play without fingers

Hold your violin from the body

Bow on the string ready to play

Step 2: To play with fingers

Hold your violin from the neck

Mr Straight (your left Thumb) should be placed between the 2 white stickers and pointing to the ceiling, hand close to the pegs

Bow on the string ready to play

From Rest Position to Playing Position

Rest Position!   **Zip!**   **Step!**   **Stop the Traffic!**

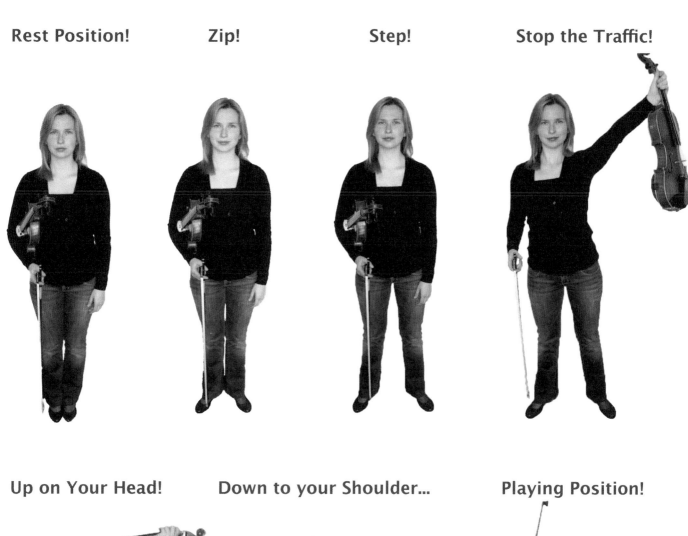

Up on Your Head!   **Down to your Shoulder...**   **Playing Position!**

Pop! Goes the Weasel

Traditional English

E - very night when I get home, the Mon - key's on the ta - ble,

pluck!

take a stick and knock it off, Pop! Goes the Wea - sel.

All a - round the cob - bler's Bench, the Mon - key chased the Wea - sel, the

pluck!

Mon - key thought it all in fun, Pop! Goes the Wea - sel.

Luisa Faraguna © 2011

Activity

1. Listen to Track 2 and clap on the Pops!
2. Take your Violin only in Rest Position. Please, leave your bow in your case for now. Place your Left Hand Pinky behind your baby string or E String. Pluck your E String with your left hand pinky on the Pops!
3. Take your Violin in Playing Position this time and pluck your E String with your left hand pinky on the Pops!
4. Finally, your first plucking will be in Rest Position and your second pluck in Playing Position. In between the plucks you will need to do very quickly the choreography in page 11. Make sure you feel the speed of the music. At the beginning, it may feel really fast but as soon as you master the movements you will

Learning Points

- Rest Position & Playing Position accuracy & transition
- Pulse feeling & Left Hand Plucking Technique
- Body coordination

Chapter 3: Beginners Bow Hold

The Beginners Bow Hold is slightly different and easier than the professionals one but really effective to start with:

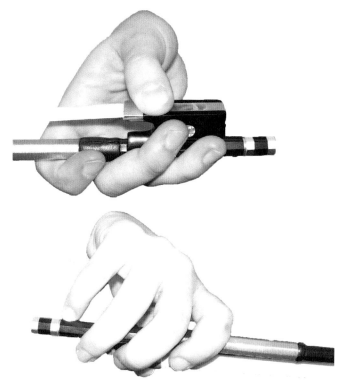

1. Open the velcro and take your bow out of your case by sliding it to your right

2. Make sure you are now holding it with your right hand

3. Bend your right hand Thumb now called Mr Bumpy on the silver part. He will stay round forever

4. Try to hide the dot with Mr Middle and Mrs Ring fingers. It does not matter if is not completely hidden but ensure that your middle and ring fingers are touching the black part called the Frog.

5. Your index should roundly cover the silver part around the stick

6. Now turn your hand around and place your Mrs Pinky on top of the stick

7. Your fingers will not be far from each other

8. Your hand should be as relaxed as possible, now you are ready to play our games!

Copycat Bow Games

Getting comfortable with the bow hold is essential. Some ideas for copycat may be: windscreen wiper blades, glasses, moustache, telephone, hunting bow, magic wand, orchestral conductor, tasty soup stirring, witches brew stirring, painting letters in the sky, through the needle, rainbow, Pinocchio liar nose, etc.

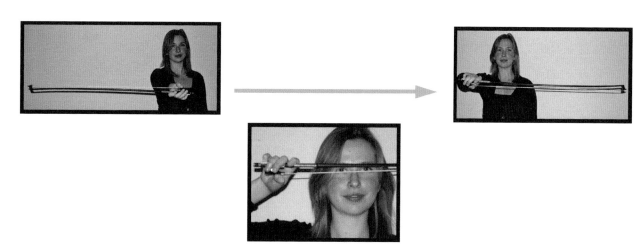

The Rocket Song

Composers: Claire & Suzannah Wake
Arranger: Luisa Faraguna

Up   like   a   Rock - et,   Down   like   the   rain,

Back   and   for - ward   like   a   choo   choo   train.

Luisa Faraguna © 2011

Activity

Sing with actions:

1. Take your bow out of your case.
2. Hold it with your right hand and your best bow hold as learned in page 13.
3. Point to the ceiling with the tip of your bow.
4. Play track 3 of you CD.
5. Sing along and move with the bow in your hand:
    5.a. pointing up with the tip first,
    5.b. then down with the frog (not the tip),
    5.c. back and forth to your left and right.

Learning Points

- Bow hold relaxation and freedom
- Singing and moving at the same time
- Coordination
- Following instructions
- Enjoying music

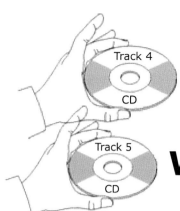

Tasty Soup

Composer: Luisa Faraguna

Witches & Wizards' Brew

Composer: Luisa Faraguna

Decide between cooking a Tasty Soup or making a magic Witches or Wizard's Brew and start with our game. Example:

Teacher: *"We are now going to cook a Tasty Soup / Witches & Wizard's Brew. Let's listen to the CD and start stirring your big pot. What ingredients would you like?"*

Students: *"Carrots!"*

Activity

Talk with actions:
1. Take your bow out of your case.
2. Hold it with your right hand and your best bow hold as learned in page 13.
3. Point to the ceiling with the tip of your bow.
4. Play track 4 of you CD.
5. Start stirring your soup with the bow in your hand.
6. Start with the cooking dialog. Students can choose as many ingredients as they like. At the end of the cooking process we pretend to drink it from our stirring bow. If it is a Tasty Soup we would make a Yummy Sound, if it is a Witches Brew we would make a Yucky Sound.

Learning Points

- Bow hold relaxation and freedom
- Talking and moving at the same time
- Independence of movements
- Imagination and creativity
- Enjoying music and having fun

Chapter 4: Violin Strings Language & Plucking

Human Book: Visual Symbols for Strings & Fingers

At this stage of music education, it is really important establishing a good violin posture. Therefore, notation is only briefly introduced with games that do not include the violin yet. The picture on the right shows a visual language of symbols for non verbal musical communication to help the children memory and concentration.

Singing and showing the Human Book Symbols at the same time is proven to be a highly effective way of learning and memorising successfully and quickly a number or songs. We remember:
10% of what we read,
20% of what we hear,
30% of what we see,
40% of what we physically do,
So, that makes 90% of what we hear, see and do at the same time!

To this symbols we can even add some finger numbers 1-4 to be played with the left hand on any of the strings (in 1st position) when required. The mirror concept applies here, I am using my right hand in the picture when students will be using their left hand to reinforce the kinaesthetic memory.

Track 6
CD

Funk Pluck!

Composer: Luisa Faraguna

2 plucks

4 plucks

8 plucks!

Activity

1. Plucking in Rest Position:

a) Hold your Violin in Rest Position (feet together)
b) Your Left Hand should hold the Violin Neck without touching the strings with your fingers.
c) Your right elbow should be on the chin-rest.
d) Make sure you are not stopping the strings from ringing with your right arm.
e) Play Track 6 on your CD
f) Make sure you play the right amount of *pizzicati* or plucks on each string.

2. Plucking in Playing Position:

a) Hold your Violin in Playing Position (feet apart)
b) Your Left Hand should hold the Violin Body without touching the strings with your fingers. Players that feel confident can hold the Violin from the Neck instead.
c) Make sure your right Thumb is at the edge of the fingerboard (back part) and you pluck the strings on the fingerboard part as they will ring nicer, easier and louder than close to the bridge. Plus you do not want to get any sticky rosin on your fingers.
d) Play Track 6 on your CD again and have fun!

Learning Points

1. New Music Vocabulary:
- The names of the Violin Strings E, A, D & G
- Plucking in Classical Music slang, which is actually old formal Italian language, it is called *PIZZICATO*. The short term for *Pizzicato* is normally written *pizz.* in music scores. Students should remember our new Italian word

2. Right Hand Plucking or *pizzicato* technique itself in both rest position and playing position

Chapter 5: Bowing on 1 String

ABCD Bow Practice

Learning to bow nicely is essential to get yummy and groovy sounds versus yucky ones right from the start. Tone quality is the main priority for every violinist from day one of lessons so... Let's get started!

'ABCD Bow Practice' is a Pre-Bowing Rhythmic Exercises System invented and named by Luisa Faraguna after years of teaching experience. We will start by placing 3 stickers on the bow:

- Top Star
- Middle Line
- Bottom Star

As you can see the Bow is now divided into 3 different sections:

- Whole Bow - from Top Star to Bottom Star and vice versa (skipping Middle Line)
- Upper Half - from Top Star to Middle Line and vice versa
- Lower Half - from Bottom Start to Middle Line and vice versa

A. Sliding finger on the Bow - Only the Bow is needed

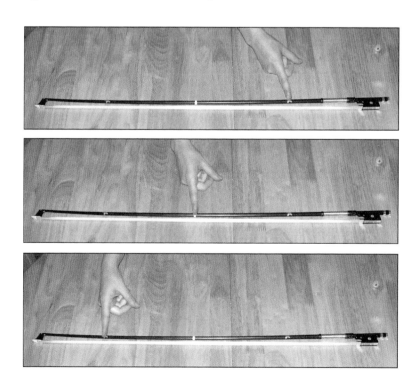

B. Soaping Arms

You only need your arms so leave your violin and bow in your case for now. This exercise can be done anywhere and it is very good practice:

C. Bow & Roll

Take a finished toilet roll and paint it! Make it look like you want to play with it!

D. Playing with Violin & Bow

You will now need:

1. Perfect Posture learned in Chapter 2 that will allow you to bow freely and easily
2. Perfect Bow Hold that we learned in Chapter 3 that will give your hand and bow the right angle over the violin to produce a healthy and pleasant sound

Amount of Bow to be Used

Rhythm Pattern	British Name	Time Length	Amount of Bow
	Quavers (tei tei tei tei)	1/2 bit	fast half bow (lower or upper)
	Crochets Triplet (ta ta ta)	2/3 bit	slow half bow (lower or upper)
	Crochets (ta ta)	1 bit	fast whole bows
	Minims (ta-a)	2 bits	slow whole bows

The right amount of straight bow at the right speed, between the bridge and finger board and with the right amount of weight will produce the fantastic sound we are looking for.

1 String Tunes Family:

eTunes!

Composer: Luisa Faraguna

eTune Watermelon

Wa - ter - me - lon   Wa - ter - me - lon
Co - ca - co - la   Pep - si - co - la
Tei   tei   tei   tei   Tei   tei   tei   tei

eTune Strawberry

Straw - ber - ry   Straw - ber - ry
Fi - ga - ro   Fi - ga - ro
Ta   ta   ta   Ta   ta   ta

eTune Apple

App - le   App - le
Ta   ta   ta   ta

eTune Pear

Pear   Pear
Taa   Taa

eTune Lemonade

Le - mon - ade Le - mon - ade
Tei   tei   ta   tei   tei   ta

eTune Blackcurrant

Black - curr - ant Black - curr - ant
Ta   tei   tei   ta   tei   tei

eTune Margherita Pizza

Margh - er - i - ta Pizz - a
Ever - y Bo - dy Down Up
Tei   tei tei tei   ta   ta

eTune This is How We End

This is How We End This is How We End clap! clap!
E - very bo - dy down, e - very bo - dy Up step! step!
tei tei tei tei ta tei tei tei tei ta shush! shush!

1 String Tunes Family:

aTunes!

Composer: Luisa Faraguna

aTune Watermelon

Wa - ter - me - lon Wa - ter - me - lon
Co - ca - co - la Pep - si - co - la
Tei tei tei tei Tei tei tei tei

aTune Strawberry

Straw - ber - ry Straw - ber - ry
Fi - ga - ro Fi - ga - ro
Ta ta ta Ta ta ta

aTune Apple

App - le App - le
Ta ta ta ta

aTune Pear

Pear Pear
Taa Taa

aTune Lemonade

aTune Blackcurrant

aTune Margherita Pizza

aTune This is How We End

Rhythms of the Strings

Composer: Luisa Faraguna

Activity

This activity applies to both One String Tunes Family (all eTunes & all aTunes) plus Rhythms of the Strings. Using the right amount of bow is essential to get the right amount of sound at this stage. We will divide the bow in Upper and Lower Half skipping the edges so we don't fall off the bow. We will then practice them using our ABCD Bow Practice:

A. Sliding finger on bow
B. Soaping rhythms
C. Bow & Roll
D. Playing with violin & bow!

Please note that fast notes will use half bows, long and slower notes will use whole bows. We will sometimes sing the rhythm patterns with half (quaver), whole (crochet) and slow (minim) as lyrics to remember how much bow we will need to use. See page 21.

1. Sing with Fruity Rhythm Names (to memorise patterns easily)
2. Sing with Tas & Teis (phonetic representation of rhythmical values)
3. Sing with Whole, Half & Slow (to remember the amount of bow needed)

Learning Points

- Reading Rhythm in both Patterns and individual figures
- Recognise rhythms aurally
- Ability to count meanwhile moving using thinking voice
- Call & Response - Action & Reaction timing
- Performance capacity
- Time feeling
- Time, space, speed connection
- Abstract concepts assimilation
- Bow control
- Bow distribution
- Coordination
- Concentration
- Adaptation

Chapter 6: Tilt your Bow

Different Strings is equal to different Bow & Right Elbow Levels

1st Floor: E String

2nd Floor: A String

3rd Floor: D String

4th Floor: G String

Activity

We are now going to practice our elbow and bow taking the lift from the 1st floor to to the 4th floor with Straight Rock & Roll and Freezing Rock & Roll Game.

Straight Rock & Roll

Composer: Luisa Faraguna

1. Place your bow in the middle over the bridge where it does not make any sound.
2. Play your CD 1, Track 24.
3. Move along the 4 floors back and forth at the speed of the music.

Freezing Rock & Roll game is also known as *Musical Statues*. Basically, when the music sounds we start lifting our elbow from the 1st to the 4th Floor and backwards.

Freezing Rock & Roll

Composer: Luisa Faraguna

We must follow the music's speed and when the music stops we freeze!

1. Place your bow in the middle over the bridge where it does not make any sound.
2. Play your CD 2, Track 24.
3. Move along the 4 floors back and forth at the speed of the music and have fun!

Learning to Play

Composer: Luisa Faraguna

Activity

ABCD Bow Practice Process. Tips:

1. Please note that line one starts on a down bow while line two starts on a down bow and has an extra long note at the end.
2. Use your thinking-singing voice for to help you count how many As you need to play.

Learning Points

- Bow directions combined with tilting the bow on E and A strings back and forth
- Playing in a group everybody with the same bow direction
- Following your leader or leading yourself the other players
- Using your thinking-singing voice
- Body Coordination
- Song structure
- Memory

Brazilian Samba

Composer: Rafael dos Santos
Arranger: Luisa Faraguna

Luisa Faraguna © 2011

Activity

While listening to CD1, track 26:

1. Clap the rhythm pattern 'Everybody Down, Everybody Up' and say 'shush' on the rests 2 rests after that. Use your singing or thinking voice if needed.
2. Clap the rhythm pattern 'Everybody Down, Everybody Up' and click your fingers twice on the rests
3. Clap the rhythm pattern 'Everybody Down, Everybody Up' and give 2 steps, first right and then left on the rests
4. ABC Bow Process stepping on the rests
5. Play the song with Violin and Bow without the steps. Make sure you tilt your bow by lifting your elbow up to the following string after playing twice the pattern.
6. Play the song with Violin, Bow and Steps on rests. Don't be late and... have fun!

Learning Points

- Instrument Exploration
- Different sounds of different strings
- Ability to recognise and react
- Song Structure
- Coordination upper and lower body
- Balance
- Relaxation
- Memory

Chapter 7: Left Hand Fingers

It is very important that by the time the students start using their left hand fingers their posture and bow hold is solid and confident. They should already been producing a healthy round sound.

What to do

1. **Water Fall** - Arm straight from your elbow to your finger tips

2. **Tunnel** - Like holding a branch in the jungle

3. **Turn** your tunnel to the left to get closer your palm and fingers closer to the strings

4. **Umbrella Fingers** - prepared to play on Finger Pattern 1 on the top of the strings

Finger Pattern 1

We have 2 stickers for Mr 1 and Mr 3. Mr 2 is best friend and neighbour of Mr 3 so the go close together. We will not use Mr 4 yet.

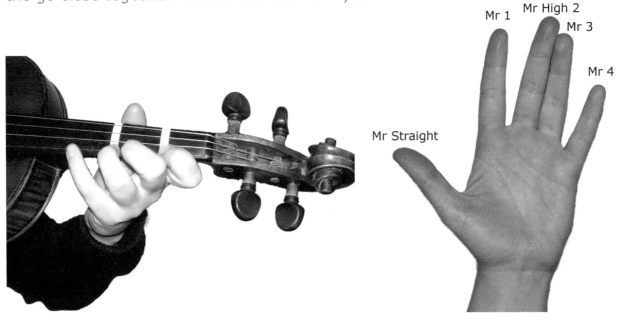

Left Hand Finger Pattern 1 Checklist

Please note that Finger Pattern 1 will apply to every song in My Beginners Book 1 so it is very important you master this:

- Check that your wrist is straight keep and therefore you show a nice Water Fall all the time.
- Mr Straight lives between the white stickers and points to the ceiling
- Mr 1 lives on the first sticker
- Mr 1 and Mr 2 are not neighbours. There is a gap between them.
- Mr 2 DOES NOT live on the second sticker but just before it.
- Mr High2 and Mr3 are best friends. They go close together to every string.
- Mr 3 lives on the second sticker
- Mr 4 stays up and round. He does not like to be squashed down so leave it up and relaxed

What to Avoid Doing

1. **Squashed Tomato or Frying Pans** - If you were holding a juicy tomato inside your hand you would get all dirty. We do not want that.

2. **Broken Wrist** - You will not be able to reach the stickers comfortably with your fingers. Please see Water Falls!

3. **Flat Fingers** - We don not like them. All your knuckles need to be round and beautiful.

4. **Pinky Squashed Down** - It creates a lot of tension in your hand. You would get really tired so keep it up and round.

Ghost Fingers

Violinists call Ghost Fingers the action of pressing the fingers down on the string without using the bow. We use this technique to practice our left hand fingers in both rest and playing position.

Monkey Song
in A Major (E String)

Composer: Claire Wake

e   e   e   e   e   1   1   1   1   1   1   2   2   2   2   2   2   3   3   3   3   3   3

I'm a lit-tle mon-key   clim-bing up the lad-der,   climbing to the top to   pick my blue ba-na - na,

3 3 3 3 3 3   2 2 2 2 2 2   1 1 1 1 1 1   e e e e e

I'm a lit-tle mon-key   clim-bing down the lad-der   clim-bing to the ground to   eat the red ba-na - na.

Monkey Song
in D Major (A String)

Composer: Claire Wake

a   a   a   a   a   a   1   1   1   1   1   1   2   2   2   2   2   2   3   3   3   3   3   3

I'm a lit-tle mon-key   clim-bing up the lad-der,   clim-bing to the top to   pick my blue ba-na - na,

3 3 3 3 3 3   2 2 2 2 2 2   1 1 1 1 1 1   a a a a a a

I'm a lit-tle mon-key   clim-bing down the lad-der   clim-bing to the ground to   eat the red ba-na - na.

Luisa Faraguna © 2011

Activity

Play your CD1, track 27 to start practicing Monkey Song on E string on the first place. Once you master playing Monkey Song on E string you can start practicing it on A string as well with track 28. This is the first song you will play with bow and fingers and you will need to do some preparatory exercises to make sure you will get it right with a pleasant sound. This steps will also apply to the next songs in the book such as Pease Pudding, Twinkle Twinkle Little Star, Old MacDonald and A Major Scale Song.

Steps for Learning Songs:

A. Left Hand

1. Sing with lyrics and actions, choose one or two crazy banana colours and remember them
2. Sing with finger numbers at the same time as you show your human book visual symbols. See page 16
3. Now take your violin in rest position without the bow and prepare your finger pattern 1 shape over E string. Sing with finger numbers as you press down your ghost fingers on the strings. Read pages 30 and 31 again if you have any doubts
4. Hold your violin in playing position and sing with finger numbers as you press your ghost fingers down

B. Right Hand

Sing the song as you practice using the right amount of bow with ABCD method without left hand fingers:

1. Sliding right hand finger on the Bow
2. Soaping Arms, right hand over left hand
3. Bow & Roll, hold the roll with left and bow with right hand
4. Playing with Violin & Bow

You can decide if you prefer singing with lyrics, finger numbers, rhythm pattern name (in this case everybody down up), or whole and half words to remember how much bow you are going to use for each note.

C. Hands Together

Once you have succeeded in steps A and B with one hand at a time, you are ready to try playing with violin and bow. If you find it very difficult it means you will need a bit more practice on A and B steps.

Learning Points

- Left hand Fingers with Finger Pattern 1
- Coordination and hands independence, doing two different things at the same time with left and right hands and arms
- Intonation accuracy - ear training
- Bowing and sound quality - using right amount of straight bow

Pease Pudding
in E Major (E String)

Traditional English
Arranger: Luisa Faraguna

Pease Pudding
in A Major (A String)

Traditional English
Arranger: Luisa Faraguna

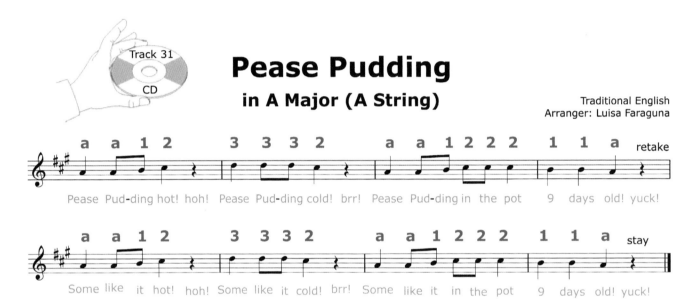

Luisa Faraguna © 2011

Activity

Please, follow the Steps for Learning Songs in page 33. Please start with Pease Pudding on E String.

Learning Points

- Retakes - circle with the bow when you finish down bow and you need to start again on a down bow
- Different bow lengths for different fingers
- Music Rests - counting time

Chapter 8: 2 String Songs

Both Monkey Song and Pease Pudding are songs on one string only. However, we have been playing them in two different keys to make them playable on both E string and A string. You can even play them on D or G string and see how they sound like. It is an excellent exercise to keep exploring the sound of your instrument. This musical concept is called transposition.

The new songs we are going to learn use two different strings which are going to be A & E strings. If you get really good at them you could also play them on other strings such as D & A or G & D.

Activity

- Follow page 33 steps again
- Make sure you play your left hand fingers on the right string whether it is A or E
- Make sure you tilt when it is due by lifting or lowing your elbow from the first to the second floors

Learning Points

- Dynamics or different sound volumes if we decide to play the second chocolate quieter than the first, eco sound effect
- Playing songs on 2 different strings with finger pattern one and tilts
- Good sound with long relaxed and straight bowing
- Block and independent fingering on bars 3 and 4
- Bow direction symbols
- Repetition
- Intonation
- Memory

Old MacDonald

Traditional American
Arranger: Luisa Faraguna

Activity

- Follow page 33 steps again
- Make sure you play your left hand fingers on the right string whether it is A or E
- Make sure you tilt when it is due by lifting or lowing your elbow from the first to the second floors

Learning Points

- Mastering songs on 2 strings
- Tilting on stopped strings (1 on A to 2 on E) instead of open strings as in Twinkle Twinkle Little Star
- Different song structure
- Memory and repetition
- Intonation

A Major Scale Song

Composer: Luisa Faraguna

Play out loud A Ma - jor Scale and prac - tice prac - tice e - very - day!

You will get a stic - ker now if you can play your scale out loud!

Play it, play it, up and down, let's make it nice with yum - my sound,

Sure that Mum - my's real - ly proud so let's get up and hug her now!

Luisa Faraguna © 2011

Activity & Leaning Points

Learn to sing and play A Major Scale Song with Recording CD1-33 and Backing Track CD2-33. Afterwards, play A Major Scale and Arpeggio as shown below in our music staves and finger pattern graphics:

A Major Scale

A Major Arpeggio

- Major Scale and Arpeggio concepts
- A Major Scale is a Grade 1 Violin Scale
- A chord is a combination of notes that are played at the same time
- An arpeggio is that combination of notes played one after the other

Chapter 9: Reading Music Notes

We have been reading rhythm and playing games with flash cards from the very beginning of lessons. This is a just short explanation about reading Pitch which may be useful to refer to at any point of the book.

Music Land

This is where we write music, also known as staff or stave:

Open Strings

If we think it is like a block of flats and count the lines and spaces from the bottom to the top, we find that all the violin strings otherwise known as open strings live in a space:

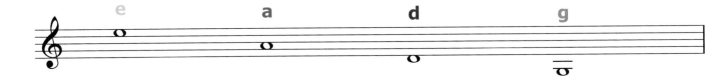

E String - Top String, Top Space
A String - Second String, Second Space
D String - Basement
G String - Minus 2 Level in the Underground

The symbol at the beginning of the stave is the Treble Clef, which is the violin language and other instruments as well such as the right hand of the piano, guitar, flute, etc. There are other clefs such as Bass Clef and Alto Clef.

Some notes can live both above and below the 5 lines of the stave. However, these notes will need to build additional lines such as G string.

Stopped String

Using fingers in first position on finger pattern 1 this is what we get from the lowest to the highest:

3 Different Languages to name the sounds
- See in Colours the violin finger numbers in first position
- See in Grey the ABC music system
- See in Black the Sol-fa music system

Printed in Great Britain
by Amazon.co.uk, Ltd.,
Marston Gate.